OVERVIEW

Overview

Communicating with a senior executive is probably not something you do every day, and you're probably glad about that. Whether by phone, e-mail, or in person, communicating with a senior executive can be a daunting and stressful challenge. But it can also be an incredible opportunity to get your point across, influence decisions, and establish yourself as someone with value to contribute. It's an opportunity you'll want to make the most of.

Given what's at stake, it's critical that you prepare this communication properly and professionally. Doing this will not only impress the senior executive, it will maximize your chances of successfully achieving the goal of the communication.

Proper preparation begins with considering the characteristics and drivers that influence a senior executive's decision-making. You also need to be clear about the parameters of your communication. What is it you want to communicate? What are you trying to achieve?

If your communication is going to succeed, you also need to follow certain other principles. For example, your message must be to the point and relevant. It must correspond to the executive's personality and decision-making style. And you need to be on top of the financial and customer implications of what you're saying.

This course will help you shape and clarify your communications with senior executives. It will outline the principles to follow and present some very important tips on building credibility with senior executives. These principles and tips are all crucial to ensure that you're taken seriously.

Finally, this course will provide detailed guidance on how best to approach and plan your meetings with senior executives. Overall, the course will help you make your communications with senior executives more productive and beneficial to all concerned.

Does the idea of communicating with senior executives in your company make your heart race, give you chills of terror, or make your mind go completely blank? Communication isn't everybody's strength, but in business, having the skills to effectively communicate your ideas to senior executives will make you a better manager.

You probably know there's a big difference between a meeting and chatting with a senior executive in the parking lot. Or between presenting a new idea to senior executives and reporting on how your project is progressing.

Communicating Effectively with Senior Executives

You must be prepared to communicate with senior executives in both formal and informal settings. You'll also explore different communication platforms like presentations, e-mail, phone calls, and elevator pitches, and learn about the advantages and disadvantages of each. Then you'll be able to use what you've learned to choose the most appropriate platform to deliver your message.

You'll also learn how to adapt your approach for different purposes depending on what you're trying to achieve with your communication. The purpose of your communication may be to report, propose, or make a request. But whatever your purpose, this course will teach you appropriate principles and guidelines to follow so you get your message across effectively.

CHAPTER 1 - PREPARING TO COMMUNICATE EFFECTIVELY AT THE 'C' LEVEL

CHAPTER 1 - Preparing to Communicate Effectively at the 'C' Level
SECTION 1 - Prepare to Communicate at the "C" Level
SECTION 2 - Principles of "C" Level Communication
SECTION 3 - Planning a Meeting with Senior Executives

SECTION 1 - PREPARE TO COMMUNICATE AT THE "C" LEVEL

SECTION 1 - Prepare to Communicate at the "C" Level

To effectively plan your communications with senior executives, you should begin by understanding them – what their characteristics and drivers are. Senior executives are high performers who are busy and under pressure, focused on results and success, short on time, and impatient with distractions. Their decisions are based on certain drivers, including financial, supplier, business partner, customer, competitor, globalization, and regulatory.

Once you understand your audience, there are certain considerations for preparing your communication. You must first be clear about what you want to communicate. Then, you must get clear about what the communication is meant to achieve. Finally, you must decide how you'll communicate.

BENEFITS OF PLANNING COMMUNICATIONS

Benefits of planning communications

How would you feel if you were asked to give a presentation to a senior executive? You'd probably be excited by the opportunity, but also nervous about the challenge. After all, communicating with a senior executive isn't the same as communicating with your manager or your peers. In order to overcome any apprehension, you'd need to prepare carefully.

Senior executives are the highest level executives in a corporation or organization. They're sometimes referred to as corporate-level – or "C" level – executives, and are part of the corporate suite, or "C" suite. They typically include positions such as the Chief Executive Officer (CEO), the Chief Operations Officer (COO), and the Chief Financial Officer (CFO).

There's a lot to consider when preparing your communication with a "C" level executive. For example, say you need to approach a CFO to get the budget for your project approved. You may be in a hurry to get approval, but communicating with the "C" level requires preparation.

You need to take time to carefully prepare your case. You'll have to present supporting data, showing why the original budget is insufficient. You'll then need to explain exactly how much of an increase is required, and what the return on this additional spending will be.

You're more likely to achieve your goals if you can show that you've prepared your case. Because you've shown that you're serious about your request, you're more likely to get serious consideration from the senior executive. By being prepared, you'll also appear more focused and engaged. This will likely help you gain respect from senior management.

Question

What are the benefits of effectively planning your communications with senior executives?

Options:

1. You're more likely to achieve your goals
2. You'll be respected by the relevant senior executive
3. You're treated more favorably or even preferentially
4. You'll be able to persuade the senior executive to make decisions that benefit you personally

Answer

Option 1: This option is correct. Only well-prepared communications get serious consideration.

Option 2: This option is correct. A prepared communication will be respected, which will reflect on you personally.

Option 3: This option is incorrect. Although there are benefits to a well-planned communication, preferential treatment is not one of them.

Sorin Dumitrascu

Option 4: This option is incorrect. A professional senior executive typically makes decisions in the interests of the organization and its strategic direction.

CONSIDERING CHARACTERISTICS AND DRIVERS

Considering characteristics and drivers

As with any communication, you should account for your audience. So when preparing to communicate with the "C" level, you should consider the typical characteristics of senior executives and the drivers of their decision-making.

Understanding the characteristics of senior executives is essential when communicating with the "C" level. If you fail to take these characteristics into account, you're unlikely to communicate successfully.

Almost all senior executives tend to be very busy and under pressure. They're also short on time. For this reason, they're unlikely to react well to being unnecessarily distracted or interrupted. Senior executives are usually focused on the bottom line. Because of their responsibilities, they want to know how you can deliver results.

In addition, they're typically high performers who are aiming for success at all times.

Question

Which are typical characteristics of senior executives?

Options:

1. Busy and under pressure
2. Eager to please
3. Impatient about distractions
4. Obstructive
5. Driven by financial results
6. High performers

Answer

Option 1: This option is correct. Senior executives tend to have busy schedules, meaning they're almost always under pressure.

Option 2: This option is incorrect. Senior executives routinely make difficult decisions. Their aim is to make the right decision, not to please people.

Option 3: This option is correct. Given their hectic schedules, senior executives tend to become impatient when distracted.

Option 4: This option is incorrect. A senior executive is no more likely to be obstructive than anyone else.

Option 5: This option is correct. Senior executives are themselves evaluated on the basis of results, so they tend to make decisions accordingly.

Option 6: This option is correct. Senior executives are accustomed to succeeding, and strive for a high level of performance.

The characteristics that are typical of senior executives are certainly important considerations when planning your communication with them. However, you also need to keep in mind the various drivers that affect senior executives. These drivers are financial, supplier, business partner, customer, competitor, globalization, and regulatory.

Financial

Senior executives are under constant pressure to improve the organization's financial performance. With this requirement constantly on their minds, nothing speaks louder than a proposal that promises to increase revenue or reduce costs.

Supplier

Senior executives are constantly looking for ways to reduce the number of suppliers they use. As well as giving greater buying power, dealing with a small number of suppliers is easier. If you've identified how your organization could benefit by changing its supply base, the senior executive will want to know.

Business partner

With the business environment constantly changing, senior executives are always keen to identify new potential business partners. They want alliances that create value for the organization. Is there a potential relationship that you could broker on the organization's behalf? If so, bring it to the attention of the relevant senior executive.

Customer

Most senior executives are focused on the organization's customers. They want to expand the customer base, and foster and improve the loyalty of existing customers. If you have an idea that can contribute in this area, you'll be regarded as someone who can help develop competitive advantage for the organization.

Competitor

In addition to traditional competitors, executives keep a close eye on marketplace trends, which can give an insight into emerging competition. If you have information that provides insight into this, share it.

Globalization

Globalization presents both challenges and opportunities, neither of which senior executives can ignore. It forces them to consider ways to reduce costs – either within the domestic infrastructure or through outsourcing. If you've assessed your organization's position and options, you may have a valuable contribution to make.

Regulatory

More so than ever before, organizations must comply with an array of regulations, many designed to ensure greater accountability and transparency. These include financial accounting compliance, labor laws, and environmental regulations. If you see ways the organization can improve its regulatory compliance, senior executives will be interested.

If you don't understand the drivers, any effort at communication will be seen as an unwelcome interruption. However, if you do, you'll be seen as a relevant and credible individual with something real and valuable to contribute.

Question

What are the key drivers that affect decision-making at the "C" level?

Options:

1. Pressure to improve financial performance and identify new business partner alliances

2. Desire to reduce the number of suppliers used and expand the customer base

3. Ensure compliance with financial accounting regulations and environmental laws

4. Ensure suppliers are paid on time to maintain positive relations

5. Monitor the competition, while considering the challenges and opportunities of globalization

6. Monitor employees' activities to ensure they're contributing to the company's bottom line

Answer

Option 1: This option is correct. Financial and business partner drivers are central to senior executives' decisions. In addition to improving financial performance, they want partner relationships that generate value.

Option 2: This option is correct. Supplier and customer drivers are key to senior executives' decisions. Reducing the number of suppliers enhances buying power, while expanding the organization's customer base increases revenue.

Option 3: This option is correct. The requirement on senior executives to ensure compliance with regulations is greater than ever before.

Option 4: This option is incorrect. While senior executives want relations with suppliers to be harmonious, this is not among their responsibilities.

Option 5: This option is correct. All senior executives are aware of competitor and globalization drivers. In addition to monitoring competitors, executives must assess the opportunities and threats posed by globalization.

Option 6: This option is incorrect. Senior executives are engaged in issues related to the organization's strategic direction, not day-to-day activities.

PREPARING TO COMMUNICATE

Preparing to communicate

Communicating with senior executives involves many challenges. However, if you take the time to carefully prepare your communication, you can increase your chances of success.

Planning your "C" level communication requires consideration of three key criteria:
- be clear about what you want to communicate,
- be clear about what you want to achieve, and
- be clear about how you'll communicate your message.

The first thing to consider in planning your communication is to decide what it is that you want to communicate. What's the content of your communication? Perhaps you're providing information, making a sales pitch, or communicating your own personal view or opinion on something.

For example, the "what" of your communication could be information. Perhaps you're a sales manager who's required to communicate the quarterly sales data to a senior executive. The information you're communicating is the sales figures.

Or the "what" could be a request. You might be seeking extra resources for a project you're managing. Alternatively, you might be communicating a proposal – an idea, a change of strategic direction, or a new product line.

Finally, you might just want to provide your opinion with regards to a particular situation or recent business decision. What you're communicating might be your opinion.

Question

Imagine you're a senior manager with a hospitality company. You've identified an unserved niche in the market and believe your company should develop a product for this niche. You share the idea with some colleagues in marketing, do some research, and pull together a quick business case for the introduction of the new product line. You communicate this to a senior executive.

What are you communicating in this case?

Options:
1. Information
2. Opinion
3. Proposal
4. Request

Answer

Option 1: This is an incorrect option. Although information might be included, this isn't the main point being communicated.

Option 2: This is an incorrect option. Although there would be some opinion, the communication is not primarily about this.

Option 3: This is the correct option. In proposing that your company develop an appropriate product, you're making a proposal.

Option 4: This is an incorrect option. You're not seeking additional resources.

The second thing to consider in planning your communication is to clarify what it is that your communication is meant to achieve. What is its purpose or goal? This could be anything from driving a decision to finding a solution to a problem.

One goal might be to influence a decision. For example, imagine you're a regional manager of a retail company with a nationwide chain of outlets. The company is currently assessing its regional markets to determine where to expand. In communicating the case for your own region, your goal would be to influence the decision.

Having done this, the goal of your next communication might be to engage in discussion. Perhaps you now want to discuss the case for your region.

You might follow up on this discussion with a communication intended to convey information. This could be in response to a request by the executive for additional details. After this, the goal of your next communication might be to plan a process. If the senior executive is convinced by your argument, you might be asked to put together a plan for the expansion.

Having put together this plan, your next goal in communicating with the executive might be to get approval for the plan. For example, you might craft a communication seeking the go-ahead for your proposed approach.

Another goal in communicating with a senior executive might be to reach a solution. Perhaps, in the implementation of your plan, you've encountered a problem. You might return to the executive to find a solution.

Question

You've compiled a plan as to how your organization could establish itself as the market leader. Although enacting the plan would require a large investment, the return would be great. You approach a senior executive to present your case.

What is the goal of this communication?

Options:

1. Influence a decision
2. Engage in discussion
3. Convey information
4. Plan a process
5. Get approval
6. Reach a solution

Answer

Option 1: This is the correct option. In presenting your case, you're attempting to influence the senior executive to make a decision in favor of your plan.

Option 2: This option is incorrect. As you're merely communicating your idea to the executive, there's no discussion underway.

Option 3: This option is incorrect. Although your approach to the senior executive will contain information, the overriding goal isn't to convey this information.

Option 4: This option is incorrect. As of yet, your idea is simply an idea. It hasn't been approved, so there's no process to plan.

Option 5: This option is incorrect. It would be premature to be seeking approval having only just communicated your idea.

Option 6: This option is incorrect. There's no problem here that requires a solution.

The third thing to consider in planning your communication is to decide how you'll communicate. The factors affecting the method of communication chosen include the content itself, its urgency, its confidentiality, and whether it's best served by being communicated orally or in writing.

A communication to a senior executive should typically be quite formal – for example, a clear, concise memo. Ultimately, the level of formality will depend on the formality or informality of the corporate culture.

It's also necessary to take account of the importance of a particular communication. If it's important, it must be communicated quickly. However, if unimportant or incomplete information is communicated in an inappropriate way, it could be seen as a distraction or interruption. This could have negative consequences.

It's a good idea to think about how and when to use the various communication mechanisms available. For example, e-mail is quick and concise, and is a good way of providing information without interrupting the recipient. However, it's not the best option when there's potential for miscommunication or when the content is sensitive or confidential.

Communicating Effectively with Senior Executives

In these cases, face-to-face communication would be better. This also enables complete communication, using body language, tone, and facial expression, and lets you respond immediately to any doubts or questions.

When face-to-face communication isn't appropriate or possible, the telephone is a good alternative. A phone call is quick and convenient. However, while it's a good way to explain things in detail, it might not be ideal for an initial communication. Unless prearranged or expected, a phone call can interrupt the recipient.

Question

You have an idea for streamlining your organization's supply base. There's no urgency, and you're aware that the senior executive in charge of supply is busy with a year-end report.

What mode of communication would be most appropriate?

Options:

1. Telephone call
2. Face-to-face meeting
3. E-mail
4. Instant message to executive's cell phone

Answer

Option 1: This option is incorrect. A telephone call is a good option when an immediate response is needed, but isn't appropriate when the issue is not urgent or when the recipient is busy.

Option 2: This option is incorrect. A face-to-face meeting is appropriate to discuss something in detail or to avoid any misunderstanding. However, in this case, the senior executive is busy and the issue is not urgent.

Option 3: This is the correct option. An e-mail is a good option to avoid interrupting the recipient. It's also appropriate as an initial contact.

Option 4: This option is incorrect. It would be inappropriate to send an instant message to an executive's cell phone unless you already have a very strong relationship or the matter is extremely important and there is no other way to contact them.

SECTION 2 - PRINCIPLES OF "C" LEVEL COMMUNICATION

SECTION 2 - Principles of "C" Level Communication

There are six principles to follow when preparing to communicate with senior executives. Your communication should be concise and relevant. It should also demonstrate a grasp of the financial implications and be customer-focused. Finally, you should be sure that your message appeals to the executive's unique decision-making style and personality type.

Getting your message across to a senior executive will largely depend on your credibility in the executive's eyes. You can build credibility by behaving and looking professional, being knowledgeable, being trustworthy, listening and being open-minded, being a problem-solver, and communicating value.

DETERMINING PRINCIPLES FOR CREDIBILITY

Determining principles for credibility

While the mere thought of communicating with senior executives might be stressful, it'll be a lot easier if you're prepared. For starters, you should familiarize yourself with the characteristics and drivers of senior executives to put yourself on their wavelength. There are also general principles for preparing to communicate with senior executives that will help you make the most of the encounter.

Perhaps you thought of the need to be succinct and relevant, or to focus on issues that matter to the executive. In fact, there are six principles that must be followed when preparing to communicate with a senior executive:

- be concise and stick to what matters,
- be sure that your message is relevant to what interests the senior executive,
- focus on the bottom line by explaining the financial implications of what you're saying,

- make sure that the focus of your message relates to customers,
- ensure you've determined the decision-making style of the executive and designed your message accordingly, and
- craft your message to appeal to the personality type of the senior executive.

The first two principles relate to the "how" and "what" of your communication. Specifically, your communication needs to be concise and relevant. The next two principles relate to the required focus of your communication. Because senior executives are focused on the financial bottom line and the customer base, it's important to appeal to these considerations.

Be concise

Because senior executives are busy, it's essential that you tell them what they need to know and no more. Don't provide historical or trivial detail, but do be prepared to give more information if requested. If your message isn't concise, there's a good chance it'll never even be considered. For example, if your main point comes in the middle of the tenth page of a 20-page document, the senior executive may not even get to it.

Be relevant

To get and hold senior executives' attention, you need to address what matters to them. By showing that you understand how they think, you'll be seen as credible and as offering something valuable. And the only way to find out what matters to senior executives is to do your homework first. Communications that lack relevancy will be ignored. For example, addressing a communication about employee morale to the CFO will likely bewilder rather than interest the executive.

Focus on the bottom line

Much of what a senior executive does is designed to increase revenues or reduce costs, which explains the constant focus on the bottom line. You need to show how your idea represents business value and how it will increase profit, either by increasing revenue or by reducing costs. An idea or proposal that will have no impact whatsoever on revenue or costs will not engage a senior executive.

Focus on customers

Senior executives care about keeping existing customers and adding new ones. They want to foster and strengthen customer loyalty. This must be central to your message. You need to show that you're also focused on customers. For example, an idea with the potential to cut costs by 50% is, in theory, great. However, have you considered the impact on customers? Would the idea significantly diminish the customer experience? If so, it may not be such a great idea in the eyes of a senior executive.

Question

Amy is a regional manager at a financial services institution. She's identified an opportunity for cost-savings in the management of the loan portfolio, the cost of which is extremely high by industry

standards. This is something the executive recently expressed interest in addressing. Implementing the change requires the approval of a senior executive, so Amy communicates her proposal in an e-mail.

Where has Amy adhered to principles for preparing to communicate with a senior executive?

Communicating Effectively with Senior Executives

Options:

1. Amy's e-mail is brief and to the point, only containing essential information

2. Amy refers to the executive's recent call for cost-cutting innovations, explaining how her proposal would reduce costs

3. Intent on covering any question that could possibly arise, Amy attaches a detailed report with an analysis of the performance of all loans over the past 25 years

4. Amy includes the findings of an analysis she conducted, showing that the company could reduce its current costs by 30%

5. While acknowledging that the changes she's proposing could have negative consequences for customers, Amy details a strategy for countering this

Answer

Option 1: This option is correct. By excluding unnecessary details, Amy's communication is concise.

Option 2: This option is correct. In addressing an issue that's of importance to the senior executive, Amy has made her message relevant.

Option 3: This option is incorrect. Senior executives are busy, and have no time for unfocused messages filled with historical data.

Option 4: This option is correct. By focusing on ways to reduce costs or increase revenue, Amy is respecting what senior executives are interested in.

Option 5: This option is correct. Senior executives are focused on customers, which includes fostering and strengthening customer loyalty. Any plan that affects customers must address this.

The final two principles relate to the tone and pitch of your communication. Different senior executives have different decision-making styles and different personality types, so you need to tailor your message to the individual executive.

Determine decision-making style

You need to determine the decision-making style of the executive and ensure your communication matches that style. Some executives make decisions on the basis of direct data and factual representations, preferring results-oriented communication. Others act in response to instinct, and prefer discussion over a quick decision. There are also some who require time to reflect before making a decision, and others who subject all proposals to a logical and systematic analysis.

Appeal to personality type

Your communication must be tailored to appeal to the specific personality type of the executive you're targeting. Is the executive a dominant, demanding type who prefers brief, direct messages over broad, general statements? Or is the executive friendly and positive, someone who wants some social interaction in any communication? Others may require patience on your part, while they cautiously process information. There are still others with logical, precise, and systematic personalities, who favor messages crafted in this way.

The executive's decision-making style should be a major factor in your chosen approach. For example, if the executive likes to reflect before making a decision, it would be inadvisable to seek a decision immediately after you have communicated your idea or proposal.

It's just as important to consider the executive's personality type. For example, if you're making a proposal to an executive who requires some social interaction in any communication, confining your approach to terse, written communications would be far from ideal.

Question

Think again of Amy, the regional manager at a financial services institution who's identified an opportunity for cost-savings in the management of the loan portfolio. She knows that the senior executive she'll be approaching makes decisions on the basis of direct data and prefers results-oriented communications. She also knows that he has a dominant, demanding personality, with little patience for broad, general statements.

Where has Amy adhered to principles for preparing to communicate with a senior executive?

Options:

1. Amy sends an e-mail that's specific and contains no vague assertions

2. Amy's e-mail includes the findings of a detailed analysis, which shows how much the company will save by implementing her proposals

3. Amy emphasizes her gut feeling that her proposal will benefit the company

4. Amy begins with her own personal bio, proving her credibility, then invites the executive to meet with her to discuss her idea

Answer

Option 1: This option is correct. Amy is adhering to the need to craft her message to the executive's personality type.

Option 2: This option is correct. Amy is taking the executive's decision-making style into account. In presenting the results of a detailed analysis, she's appealing to his preference for results-oriented communication.

Option 3: This option is incorrect. Given the executive's decision-making style, claims supported by only a strong feeling will be ignored.

Option 4: This option is incorrect. The senior executive has a demanding personality, and wants others to get to the point. Amy's indirect approach would irritate.

APPLYING PRINCIPLES FOR CREDIBILITY

Applying principles for credibility

Getting your message across to senior executives requires persuasiveness. A cornerstone of persuasiveness is credibility. But building credibility with senior executives is not as straightforward as with colleagues or friends. You're unlikely to be interacting with them regularly, offering less opportunity to make an impression. There are six principles for achieving credibility that will position you to present a persuasive argument: behave and look professional, be knowledgeable, be trustworthy, listen and be open-minded, be a problem-solver, and communicate value.

Behave and look professional

Unless you behave and look professional, you won't be regarded as professional. This extends beyond surface impressions. It's important to be courteous and respectful toward everyone you encounter. Take the time to understand things before trying to be understood; this means listening more than talking.

Be knowledgeable

Credibility grows out of being knowledgeable. You should research all you can about an issue before you communicate about it. Instead of focusing only on the argument's strengths, know its weaknesses too. Cite trusted sources or endorsements that bolster your case. You should also be able to demonstrate and prove your idea. If there's terminology unique to the area, be sure you know it.

Be trustworthy

If you're regarded as trustworthy, you'll also be seen as genuine, believable, and reliable. The flip side of this is that if you're regarded as untrustworthy, people will disregard what you say. You can earn trust by keeping your promises and respecting confidences, respecting others' opposition or concerns, being up-front about the pros and cons of your proposal, and putting others' interests ahead of your own.

Listen and be open-minded

Listening is not the same as hearing. Listening is an active process; it means understanding, interpreting, and evaluating what's being said. Being unable to listen properly damages credibility. It's equally important to keep an open mind – open to other people, new opportunities, and new ways of doing things.

Be a problem-solver

You'll boost your credibility if you get a reputation for addressing problems head-on and solving them. You'll be seen as a dependable "doer." However, if you're seen as someone who concedes at the first sign of a challenge, your credibility will take a hit.

Communicate value

Communicating Effectively with Senior Executives

Senior executives want ideas and information that have strategic and creative value. Flashy presentations, attention-seeking gimmicks, and useless, generic information will irritate busy executives. Don't waste their time. Ensure you have something real and valuable to contribute.

Consider the example of Frank, a manager with a hotel group. In response to a proposal he submitted to Audrey, the senior executive with responsibility for marketing, Frank has been invited to a meeting with her.

Frank spends the day before the meeting rereading his proposal, to ensure it's fresh in his mind, and rehearsing his opening pitch. Usually, Frank wears business attire, but, as the meeting is scheduled for Friday – a day when everyone in Frank's office dresses casually – Frank opts for khakis and a short-sleeve shirt.

Although Frank knows he'll probably be asked to provide more detail, he doesn't conduct additional research. This is partly because it sounds as if Audrey's already convinced.

How did Frank do in terms of behaving and looking professional? He certainly started well by reviewing his proposal and rehearsing his pitch. But Frank lost some credibility in other areas. For instance, it was inappropriate for him to dress so casually when meeting with a senior executive. Audrey may have thought this was unprofessional.

Also, Frank knew that he'd be required to give more detail and supporting evidence. Not preparing for this suggests complacency and, perhaps, negligence. He missed the opportunity to show he was knowledgeable.

Question

Where have the principles for communicating with a senior executive been applied?

Options:

1. Demonstrating authority, Max ignores the senior executive's personal assistant when arriving for a meeting

2. Although Betty knows little about a certain issue, she covers this by using broad, general terms

3. Before communicating his ideas, George researches his idea thoroughly

4. Despite having expertise on a particular issue, Loretta spends more time listening than talking during the meeting

Answer

Option 1: This option is incorrect. Being professional means treating everyone with respect.

Option 2: This option is incorrect. It's critical to know what you're talking about. You can't fake knowledge.

Option 3: This option is correct. To be knowledgeable, it's essential to research.

Option 4: This option is correct. Being professional includes taking the time to understand things before trying to make yourself understood.

Frank's meeting with Audrey begins well. She's clearly impressed with his well-prepared opening presentation.

After this presentation, Audrey asks if Frank anticipates any obstacles. Although he does have some doubts, he keeps them to himself, as he wants to get Audrey's approval first.

Audrey then asks Frank about one specific aspect of his plan. She queries his proposed approach, suggesting an alternative. Although Frank doesn't understand the suggestion, he rejects it and becomes defensive. He wonders whether Audrey is trying to take control of things.

In denying that there were any difficulties, Frank wasn't honest. An important component of building credibility is being trustworthy. Frank could have demonstrated his trustworthiness by acknowledging that there could be problems and suggesting potential solutions.

Another important component of building credibility is being open-minded. Frank misinterpreted Audrey's effort to assist him as a self-interested ploy, and rejected the suggestion. This showed a degree of closed-mindedness on Frank's part, and is unlikely to have impressed Audrey.

Question

Where have principles of preparing to communicate with senior executives been applied?

Options:

1. Occasionally, Jane makes promises she knows she'll be unable to keep in order to be involved in everything

2. To sustain the momentum that's gathered behind his ideas, Don politely dismisses others' concerns and doubts

3. Katerina devotes an equal amount of time to discussing both the pros and the cons of her idea

4. Despite being confident in his ideas, Nick is interested in hearing others' doubts and queries

Answer

Option 1: This option is incorrect. Failure to deliver on commitments damages others' perception of your trustworthiness.

Option 2: This option is incorrect. Being open-minded means encouraging the exploration of ideas and being open to others' perspectives.

Option 3: This option is correct. Telling both sides of the story and being honest about potential difficulties is part of being trustworthy.

Option 4: This option is correct. Keeping an open mind is an important component of building credibility.

Despite Frank's denial that he foresees any obstacles, Audrey identifies several. Fortunately, these are all issues that Frank had already considered when preparing his proposal. He offers several possible solutions to each potential problem.

Toward the end of the meeting, Audrey asks Frank about the revenue-generating potential of his idea. This is the moment Frank has been waiting for. He's prepared an impressive-looking slideshow presentation on this aspect of his proposal.

It's a 20-minute long presentation, containing colorful charts and eye-catching graphics, with a good mix of font styles and sizes. Frank put a lot of time into how the presentation looked, but only to disguise its lack of substance.

Being seen to be a problem-solver is an important component in building credibility, and Frank did well here. He suggested a range of possible solutions to the potential challenges brought up by Audrey. This impressed her.

However, it's also important to communicate value. This means giving real, credible, and results- oriented information. Frank erred in not gathering data on the revenue-generating potential of his idea. He was wrong, too, in attempting to conceal this shortcoming by dazzling Audrey with meaningless graphics.

Question

Where have the principles related to being a problem-solver and communicating value been applied?

Options:

1. When a problem arises, Ayana focuses on something else, as it's better to move forward than to waste time

2. Enrique is known for his innovative and original ideas, but has little interest in determining their practical use

3. Everyone knows that Valerie is the person to go to whenever there's a problem

4. Interested in credible, results-oriented information, Stan has no patience for generic information presented with gimmicks

Answer

Option 1: This option is incorrect. Someone who concedes defeat at the first challenge is not a problem-solver, which is part of building credibility.

Option 2: This option is incorrect. To be seen as credible, you must communicate value. Ideas that have no practical application are pointless.

Option 3: This option is correct. Those who cultivate reputations as "doers" and problem-solvers will gain credibility.

Option 4: This option is correct. Communicating value is an important part of building credibility. If information has no value, it's a waste of time.

SECTION 3 - PLANNING A MEETING WITH SENIOR EXECUTIVES

SECTION 3 - Planning a Meeting with Senior Executives

Having secured a meeting with a senior executive, it's critical to ensure it goes well. First, this requires you to properly plan the content and sequence of the meeting. There are three steps involved: determine the purpose of the meeting, determine the desired outcome or objective of the meeting, and develop a meeting agenda.

Second, you need to consider how you'll conduct the meeting. The three stages to a properly conducted meeting with a senior executive are the initial introduction, a discussion of the issues and implications, and an attempt to secure follow-up.

PLANNING THE CONTENT

Planning the content

When you've secured a meeting with a senior executive, it's important to make the most of it. That means planning the content and sequence of the meeting properly. A properly planned meeting saves time, solves problems, and generates momentum. A badly planned meeting, however, wastes time and resources, and can, in fact, be worse than no meeting at all.

Preparing the content of a meeting with a senior executive involves three steps:

- to begin with, you need to determine the purpose of the meeting,
- you then need to determine the desired outcome or objective of the meeting, which means being clear about what you want the meeting to achieve, and
- finally, you need to develop a meeting agenda, which can be understood as the "road map" to bring the meeting to its destination.

The first step in planning an effective meeting with a senior executive is to determine the meeting's purpose. The purpose of the meeting could be to provide information, engage in discussion, ask for feedback, generate ideas, solve a problem, or make a decision. It's critical that there's a clear purpose to the meeting – if not, you shouldn't have the meeting at all.

For example, say you're the product development manager of an electronics company. You're about to meet with your CEO to discuss the implications of a competitor's new product. You're concerned that your competitor now has a significant competitive advantage over your company.

The main purpose of the meeting is to provide information. You want to alert your CEO to the details and significance of the competitor's product.

However, the meeting also has other purposes. You need to discuss the implications of this development for your company. And you must also generate ideas or make decisions about how your company can counter this threat.

Question

Betty is the investment manager of a pension fund. She's concerned that the fund is overexposed to property investment. She meets with the CFO to discuss the need to alter the fund's overall strategy, and also to suggest the need to review the fund's general strategy.

What would be the purposes of this meeting?

Options:

1. To brief the CFO on the fund's level of exposure to property investment
2. To generate ideas for new pension products

3. To decide on the fund's investment strategy
4. To report on the fund's overall performance

Answer

Option 1: This option is correct. One of Betty's purposes is to present information on the fund's overexposure to the property market.

Option 2: This option is incorrect. Although generating ideas could be the purpose of some meetings, it's not in this instance. Betty's purpose is to convey information and make a decision.

Option 3: This option is correct. One of Betty's purposes is to request the CFO's approval for altering the fund's strategy, which entails a decision on the part of the CFO.

Option 4: This option is incorrect. Although this could be the purpose of some meetings, it is not in this instance.

Having determined the meeting's purpose, you next need to clarify its specific aim or objective. Clearly, this will be closely related to the purpose, but whereas the purpose is the reason you want the meeting, the objective is the outcome you want to achieve. The objective could be to get a specific decision made, get the executive's feedback or ideas on a distinct issue, find a solution to a certain problem, or discuss a particular policy, strategy, or project.

In the example of the meeting with the CEO, there are a number of objectives. One objective is to provide information to the CEO about the competitor's activities and discuss the particular implications for your company.

However, your main objective would likely be to get the CEO to provide additional funds to your own company's product development plans. So, in this case, the objective would be to get a specific decision made.

Question

Remember Betty, the pension fund investment manager who's concerned about the fund's overexposure to property investment? Betty is meeting with the CFO about the fund's investment strategy.

What are Betty's specific objectives of this meeting?

Options:

1. Impress upon the CFO that her predecessor did a poor job

2. Influence the executive to sanction an amendment to the fund's strategy

3. Get agreement that the overall strategy needs to be reviewed

4. Demonstrate her competence in identifying the overexposure

Answer

Option 1: This option is incorrect. Although this may occur to the executive, it's not Betty's objective.

Option 2: This option is correct. Betty is looking for the executive's approval to change the strategy.

Option 3: This option is correct. In addition to the immediate change, Betty wants the executive to agree to a more general review of the strategy.

Option 4: This option is incorrect. While the executive may be impressed with Betty's astuteness in identifying the problem, this shouldn't be her aim.

The final stage is developing an agenda. You'll have limited time, so you may not be able to cover everything. It's best to put urgent matters toward the top of the agenda to ensure they're addressed. If an issue must be skipped, it's better that it's non-urgent. Issues that can be handled quickly should also be placed high on the agenda. If these are placed behind something that'll take time to discuss, you may never get to them.

Returning to the example of your meeting with the CEO, think about how you'd put together the agenda for the meeting. To do this, you'd have to consider the purpose and the objectives.

You believe your company needs to improve its product development program, and your main objective is to get the CEO to make the required funds available for this. So you should put this at the top of your agenda.

Other issues of less importance can then be discussed after the main agenda item. Such issues might include a discussion of the technical specifications of your competitor's new product.

Question

Think again about Betty, the pension fund investment manager who's meeting with her CFO to discuss the fund's overexposure to property investment.

What issues should Betty place at the top of the meeting's agenda?

Options:

1. The general outlook for the property market
2. Her expectations for the coming three-year period
3. The degree of overexposure and the potential ramifications
4. The more general lack of balance within the overall strategy

Answer

Option 1: This option is incorrect. Although this may be of interest to the executive, it's not a pressing matter for discussion at this meeting.

Option 2: This option is incorrect. Although important, this is not an urgent issue for discussion. It should be placed at the bottom of the agenda or dealt with in a later meeting.

Option 3: This option is correct. This issue is both important and urgent, and so should be placed at the top of the agenda.

Option 4: This option is correct. Although not particularly urgent, this is important. It should be placed toward the top of the agenda.

CONDUCTING THE MEETING

Conducting the meeting

Having carefully planned the sequence and content of the meeting with a senior executive, it's time to think about how you'll conduct the meeting. To ensure you conduct a meeting with a senior executive properly, there are three stages to consider.

The meeting should begin with an initial introduction. Then, after the introduction, the second stage should be a discussion of issues and implications. In the third stage, at the close of the meeting, you should find a way to ensure some follow-up.

Introduction

In the introduction stage, you should briefly cover all aspects of the meeting. First, refer to the initial contact you made with the executive, perhaps mentioning whoever referred you.

You might then offer a brief overview of your past experience or qualifications – provided that it's relevant to what's being discussed. It's also important to be clear about the mutual benefit that you expect the meeting to deliver.

Above all, make the introduction clear and compelling.

Issues and implications

You'll spend most of the meeting discussing the issues and implications. This is when you'll demonstrate your understanding of the issues that most interest the executive.

Asking the right questions is a good way to demonstrate your understanding. Having done so, listen intently to the answers. Asking and listening enables you to assess the importance and urgency of issues, and provides insight into the executive's openness to change.

You'll then be well placed to communicate the value you can contribute.

Follow-up

Toward the end of the meeting, be sure to suggest that the executive be involved in a follow-up meeting. Give a firm indication as to how the initiative might move forward, and ask for the executive's involvement in this.

Even if the senior executive suggests that you continue the discussion with a lower-level executive or manager, you should still suggest reconnecting with the senior executive to provide an update or review of developments.

For example, Virginia is meeting with Beth, a senior executive, to discuss her proposal to modernize the company's manufacturing process. In her initial communication, Virginia suggested that installing more modern technology would reduce costs by 30%. Follow along on the coming pages as we analyze Virginia's performance during the meeting.

During her introduction, Virginia refers to her initial communication, reminding Beth of the potential benefits. She explains that her confidence in her proposal is based on her previous experience of implementing a similar change in her last job. When discussing the issues and implications, Virginia asks Beth about the intensifying competitiveness within the industry and the reasons why the company's costs are significantly above average.

Having discussed the issues and implications in detail, Virginia proposes how they might move forward with her idea. She suggests that she contact an expert consultant in the area of manufacturing methods and, based on the expert's advice, compile a plan of action to be discussed at a follow-up meeting. Finally, she asks whether Beth would be available should she require guidance while compiling this plan of action.

So how did Virginia do in conducting her meeting with Beth? Pretty well. She began with an initial introduction, ensuring that Beth was aware of her credentials and past success. She made sure, too, that Beth was aware of the benefits of her idea, making it clear that she's contributing value.

When it came to discussing the issues and implications, Virginia had clearly done her homework. She was able to ask probing, pertinent questions about the increasing competitiveness within the industry and the particular challenges this presents to her company. This is an area of concern to Beth, and Virginia showed that she understands it. Virginia also had a clear idea about how the initiative might move forward and successfully secured the involvement of Beth in this process.

Case Study: Question 1 of 3

Scenario

You're meeting with Donald, a senior executive, to discuss your proposal to transform the company's manufacturing process. Your idea is that by ensuring the manufacturing process adheres to the highest ethical and environmentally sustainable standards, the company would be favorably placed to secure lucrative government business. In addition, being able to promote and market products as "ethical" would represent a major source of competitive advantage and differentiation.

Plan the conduct of the meeting. Answer the questions in order.

Question

How would you handle the introduction?

Options:

1. Discuss the importance of environmental sustainability to the future of mankind

2. Outline your past successes in transforming brands into "ethical" and "sustainable" leaders

3. Be honest about your inexperience, but assure Donald of your enthusiasm

4. Explain how the brand will benefit from being seen as ethical and environmentally sustainable

Answer

Option 1: This option is incorrect. While this may be true, it's not appropriate for the introduction to your meeting.

Option 2: This option is correct. It's good practice to begin the meeting by providing a brief overview of your past experience or qualifications.

Option 3: This option is incorrect. If you don't have directly relevant experience or qualifications, you should consider how the experience or qualifications that you do have could be applied.

Option 4: This option is correct. The benefits that you anticipate deriving from the initiative should be introduced early in the meeting.

Case Study: Question 2 of 3

How should you approach the discussion of the issues and implications?

Options:

1. As this is the first meeting, it would be inappropriate to go into such detail

2. Demonstrate assertiveness by presenting your proposal through a commanding lecture

3. Ask a lot of questions based on the research you did prior to the meeting

4. Listen intently to what Donald has to say

Answer

Option 1: This option is incorrect. In fact, more time should be devoted to discussion of the issues and implications than anything else.

Option 2: This option is incorrect. It's necessary to demonstrate understanding of the issues facing Donald by asking questions and listening to the answers.

Option 3: This option is correct. Asking the right questions shows that you have an understanding of the issues.

Option 4: This option is correct. Listening to Donald's answers enables you to glean the executive's priorities, concerns, and willingness to implement change.

Case Study: Question 3 of 3

How would you ensure appropriate follow-up?

Options:

1. Show respect for Donald's seniority by saying you've taken the idea as far as you can and will now leave it to him

2. Demonstrate ownership of your idea by assuring Donald that no further involvement on his part will be required

3. Suggest a plan of action for how you see the idea progressing

4. Propose that you reconnect with Donald to provide an update on developments

Answer

Option 1: This option is incorrect. Your aim should be to demonstrate that you have a valuable contribution to make going forward.

Option 2: This option is incorrect. It's important to extract a commitment from Donald to be involved in the initiative as it moves forward.

Option 3: This option is correct. Executives favor processes that have a definitive outcome.

Option 4: This option is correct. Even if Donald sees no direct personal role in the initiative, it's a good
idea to suggest reconnecting later for the purposes of review, update, or guidance.

CHAPTER 2 - TECHNIQUES FOR COMMUNICATING EFFECTIVELY WITH SENIOR EXECUTIVES

CHAPTER 2 - Techniques for Communicating Effectively with Senior Executives

SECTION 1 - GENERAL PRINCIPLES OF UPWARD COMMUNICATION

SECTION 1 - General Principles of Upward Communication

When interacting with senior executives, you need to apply the four principles of effective upward communication. These will help increase your chances of success.

Make sure you've considered the senior executives' perspective. Always be respectful of their time and availability. Be focused and concise in your presentation. And, most importantly, answer questions honestly.

PRINCIPLES FOR EFFECTIVE COMMUNICATION

Principles for effective communication

Have you ever chatted with the CEO as you both leave the office at the end of the day? If you had to make a formal presentation to that same CEO, you'd probably take a different approach. Being effective at upward communication, or communication with senior executives, requires you to apply good communication principles and adapt them to any setting.

Your response may have included some or all of these four principles for effective upward communication: consider their perspective, be respectful, be focused and concise, and be honest.

There's one other consideration in upward communication – the setting, or context, for the communication. For instance, think about the difference between delivering a one-time report to a senior executive versus weekly project reports.

Sorin Dumitrascu

And if you've ever had to give bad news to a senior executive, you know the context of that message is very different than simply providing a status update.

APPLYING COMMUNICATION PRINCIPLES

Applying communication principles

The first principle of upward communication with senior executives is to consider their perspective. This enables you to empathize with them, put yourself in their position, and prepare yourself from that viewpoint. Ensure you speak their language instead of yours; it's not a time for technical or business jargon, but for clarity. And anticipate their questions, so you'll be better able to respond with precision and credibility.

Consider Brenda, who recently gave a presentation to senior executives on the findings of her office ergonomics assessment. She enthused about the ergonomically correct chair she wanted and began a lengthy slideshow of photos of recommended equipment. Halfway through the presentation, she left to get upholstery samples. And when asked questions she wasn't prepared for, her answers were based mostly on conjecture.

Brenda made the common mistake of bringing only her ideas about the ergonomic assessment and her excitement about those ideas to the meeting. She was excited about the chairs and fabrics, but the executives were focused on the time and cost it would take to upgrade the equipment.

If Brenda had applied the first principle – consider their perspective – she would've thought about what the senior executives would be interested in. She might have made a better impression by presenting only the time and costs required to implement her recommendations.

Question

How might you apply the "consider their perspective" principle of upward communication?

Options:

1. Empathize with senior executives
2. Speak their language
3. Anticipate their questions
4. Visualize their surroundings
5. Consider your own background

Answer

Option 1: This option is correct. Empathizing with senior executives helps you prepare from their perspective.

Option 2: This option is correct. Speaking their language ensures you avoid using technical jargon and are clear.

Option 3: This option is correct. Anticipating their questions will help you focus your approach and be better prepared.

Option 4: This option is incorrect. Visualizing senior executives' physical surroundings is not a part of considering their perspective.

Option 5: This option is incorrect. Reviewing your own background does not account for the perspective of others.

The second principle for effective upward communication is to be respectful. When communicating, always be respectful with regard to time, preparation, and company hierarchy.

Time

Keep in mind that time is valuable to senior executives. It's important to show respect by not wasting their time.

Preparation

You show respect for your audience by the quality of your preparation. Your presentation should be tailored to the needs and interests of the senior executives. You should provide them with notes ahead of time. And you should also ask if they'd like your full presentation or just the key points.

Company hierarchy

The position of the executive in the company hierarchy should be considered from a cultural perspective. Some cultures view senior executives differently, and the company structure may also be different from what you're used to. Make sure your approach shows an appropriate level of respect.

Recall Brenda's ergonomic assessment presentation. She presented a lengthy slideshow and even left the room halfway through the presentation to retrieve upholstery samples.

Brenda's mistake was in not recognizing the value of her audience's time. Her presentation was too long, and leaving the room make her seem ill-prepared. While she may not have meant to be, Brenda appeared disrespectful of the senior executives.

If Brenda had been applying the principle of being respectful, she would have created a brief presentation highlighting just the key points of the assessment – time and cost.

Question

When applying the principle "be respectful," what should you consider to ensure effective upward communication?

Options:

1. Time
2. Preparation
3. Company hierarchy
4. Your goal
5. Audience's education

Answer

Option 1: This option is correct. Time is valuable to busy and stressed senior executives and wasting it is disrespectful.

Option 2: This option is correct. You show respect for your audience by the quality of your preparation. You'll be able to adapt your presentation to the needs and interests of the senior executives you're addressing.

Option 3: This option is correct. Considering the hierarchy of a company's senior executives will ensure your approach correctly reflects the necessary level of respect.

Option 4: This option is incorrect. While keeping your goal in mind is important, it's not a part of applying the principle "be respectful."

Option 5: This option is incorrect. Considering the level of education of your audience is not a part of applying the principle "be respectful."

The third principle in upward communication is being focused and concise. Senior executives are constantly under time pressure and focused on the bottom line, so you must be direct. Make sure you know your communication objective and stay focused on it. If you can condense your full presentation into 30 seconds, you won't miss out on your chance if the senior executive you're talking to gets called away two minutes into your meeting.

Make a few inquiries before your meeting. Asking senior executives ahead of time what information is most important to them and what their preferred type of communication is helps ensure your presentation meets expectations.

Also, bring notes, even if you're well practiced. They'll help you remain focused, concise, and confident during your presentation.

During her presentation, Brenda made the mistake of talking for too long, and she focused on what was interesting to her, not on what the senior executives were interested in.

If Brenda had applied the principle of being focused and concise, she would have kept her presentation brief and focused on the objective – how much upgrading to ergonomic office equipment would cost. She should have provided everyone with the cost breakdown for the recommended pieces of equipment and skipped the photos and upholstery samples.

Question

How would you apply the principle "be focused and concise" in communicating with senior executives?

Options:

1. Be direct
2. Know your objective

3. Demand honesty
4. Make inquiries
5. Bring notes
6. Create visuals

Answer

Option 1: This option is correct. One simple way of being focused and concise is to express your point directly. Senior executives don't have time to puzzle over what you're getting at.

Option 2: This option is correct. It's not possible to be focused if you don't know exactly what your objective is in communicating with the senior executive.

Option 3: This option is incorrect. Demanding honesty is not a part of applying the principle "be focused and concise."

Option 4: This option is correct. Asking questions will ensure your presentation delivers what's expected when applying the principle "be focused and concise."

Option 5: This option is correct. It's a good idea to have your notes with you to help you stay focused when applying the principle "be focused and concise."

Option 6: This option is incorrect. Creating visuals is not a part of applying the principle "be focused and concise."

While the fourth principle – be honest – seems the simplest, it may be the hardest to accomplish. When asked a question, if you don't know the answer, don't make something up or try to guess. All this does is hurt your credibility and make you appear unreliable. Answer the question honestly and simply say you don't know. However, assure your audience that you'll find out and get back to them with an answer as soon as possible.

Communicating Effectively with Senior Executives

Recall how Brenda resorted to making up answers to questions, rather than relying only on the facts when formulating her responses. If Brenda had applied the fourth principle, be honest, she would have admitted she didn't know the answers. She should have simply said, "I don't know, but I'll get back to you."

In the eyes of the senior executives, her credibility was already shaken by the lack of respect and focus, and her lack of honesty reduced her reliability even further.

Question

Brad is making a report to senior executives on a proposed new health insurance plan.

Which statements about Brad's approach indicate he has applied the principles for upward communication?

Options:

1. Brad considers what executives might be most interested in and presents those facts

2. Brad times his presentation to be a little less than ten minutes

3. Brad is able to explain his objective in under a minute if necessary

4. Brad anticipates some questions and he's prepared to admit it when he doesn't know the answer

5. Brad speaks from the heart with confidence

6. Brad wants to show his expertise, so he uses mainly technical terms

Answer

Option 1: This option is correct. In considering what the key points might be from the senior executives' view, Brad was applying the principle "consider their perspective."

Option 2: This option is correct. Brad kept his presentation brief, aware that the senior executives' time was valuable. By doing so, he applied the principle "be respectful."

Option 3: This option is correct. Brad's ability to explain his objective briefly shows that he has applied the "be focused and concise" principle.

Option 4: This option is correct. Brad is honest about not knowing the answers to some of the senior executives' questions, applying the "be honest" principle.

Option 5: This option is incorrect. While confidence is a good thing, Brad could end up going off track. He may need to apply the principle "be focused and concise."

Option 6: This option is incorrect. Brad thinks using technical terms will show his expertise. But he should be speaking the senior executives' language and applying the principle "consider their perspective."

SECTION 2 - DIFFERENT COMMUNICATION PLATFORMS AND SETTINGS

SECTION 2 - Different Communication Platforms and Settings

It's important to know how to adapt your communications with senior executives, because not all platforms and settings lend themselves to the same kind of communication. You must be able to choose the right combination of attributes in communication platforms. Decide whether your approach should be formal or informal and face-to-face or electronic.

You should also review the advantages and disadvantages of each communication platform to further ensure you're choosing the best vehicle for your message. Depending on the platform you choose – for example an elevator pitch or a presentation – you must be sure to follow the associated guidelines for truly effective upward communication.

COMMUNICATION PLATFORMS AND SETTINGS

Communication platforms and settings

When you communicate with senior executives, you need to consider your method of communication – your platform – and your setting. You can't give a presentation in an elevator. You can't read body language over the phone. You can't see the instant effect of a message when you e-mail. When you know what you want to achieve from your communication, you can better choose the right platform and setting.

When planning your communication with senior executives, you can choose from a variety of platforms. These include phone, e-mail, instant messaging, face-to-face, letters, or memos. In turn, the communications guidelines you apply will depend on the platform you use. For example, you need to be especially concise when communicating via instant message.

You may have noted that it's important to adapt your communications using different platforms and in a variety of settings. You should also be aware that not all platforms and settings lend themselves to the same types of communication.

If you had to communicate an update to senior management, for example, you might be able to do it in a concise message during a conference call. Or you might detail the update in an e-mail. Or you might decide to expand on each part of the update using a half-hour presentation.

You must come to understand what works and what doesn't work in different platforms and settings. If you take the time to carefully consider these issues, you're more likely to deliver your message effectively.

COMMUNICATION PLATFORM EXAMPLES

Communication platform examples

As you're preparing your upward communication approach, think about the possible communication platforms and settings that will be most effective. It might be a tough decision, since there's a wide variety of communication platforms to choose from.

When communicating with senior executives, you can choose from two categories of communication platforms to convey your message: face-to-face and electronic. As well, within each platform category you can decide whether it's more appropriate to communicate formally or informally.

Face-to-face

Face-to-face communication platforms involve speaking to senior executives in person. For example, formal face-to-face platforms include meetings, briefing sessions, networks, and presentations. Informal face-to-face platforms include conferences, workshops, retreats, hallway chats, and elevator pitches.

Electronic

Electronic communication platforms involve delivering your message electronically. You should note that with a facilitator, an electronic presentation is considered formal face-to-face, making it the only platform that falls into both categories. Examples of informal electronic platforms are phone, e-mail, video conference, text or instant message, voicemail, message boards, and webinars.

Question

Match each example with the appropriate communication platform. Each category will have more than one match and examples may match to more than one category.

Options:

A. You schedule a briefing session with senior executives

B. You facilitate a slide presentation for senior executives

C. You run an idea by a senior executive in an elevator

D. You e-mail senior executives a budget update

Targets:

1. Face-to-face
2. Electronic

Answer

Any communication in person with senior executives belongs to this category. A briefing session or presentation are formal instances, and an elevator meeting is an informal instance.

Any case where the communication is conveyed through an electronic media belongs here. E-mail is an informal instance, and a presentation is a formal one.

COMMUNICATION PLATFORM CHARACTERISTICS

Communication platform characteristics

So being able to identify the different categories of communication platforms – face-to-face or electronic – can help you narrow down which type of platform to use in a particular setting. Next, to really help you decide which communication platform will work best, you should consider the characteristics of individual platforms.

Communication platforms have a number of characteristics:
- the level of interactivity the platform provides,
- the reliability of the platform when sending and receiving messages,
- the platform's ability to convey rich messages that incorporate emotion and tone, and
- the platform's ability to retrieve content at a later date.

Then you can use your knowledge of these characteristics to compare platforms and discover their advantages and disadvantages. The most common platforms are phone, e-mail, text messages, instant messaging, and presentations.

Phone

The phone is a very interactive platform, especially when used one-on-one. It enables back and forth conversation, and you can detect the other person's tone of voice. It's very reliable, and good at conveying rich messages.

You can quickly exchange information over the phone. However, you can retrieve content only if you use a recording device.

The phone's ability to convey rich messages can be improved upon if a conversation is used in conjunction with documents.

E-mail

E-mail is a fairly interactive platform, but can be limited by the writer's willingness to express himself and by the lack of tone. It's reliable, depending on how often the recipient checks messages, and you can always request a notification on receipt.

You can send e-mails with attachments, so the platform is good for conveying rich messages. And finally, e-mail allows messages to be retrieved anytime, as long as the sender or recipient hasn't deleted them.

E-mail is also good when use to receive feedback. And the ability to convey rich messages is best for prepared statements.

Text messages

The interactivity level of text messages is limited. Large groups can't text back adequate feedback, and small group messages are limited by word count.

If recipients have their phones on, text messaging can be very reliable. But if you're hoping to convey a rich message, texting is very limited. And although you can retrieve past texts, you're limited by the phone's memory.

Instant messaging

Instant messaging, or IM, has limited interactivity. Having to type everything delays the message, and emoticons are no substitute for face-to-face interaction.

Since your message is visible as you type, this is a reliable platform, but it's limited if you're trying to convey a rich message. And you can only retrieve messages if you've set up your IM program to keep message logs.

Presentation

Presentations have different pros and cons depending on if there's a presenter or not. The interactivity level is very good with a presenter, but limited without. With a presenter to guide the audience through the slides, it's a very reliable platform. Without a presenter though, the slides are left up to the individual's interpretation.

Presentations allow you to convey rich messages. With a presenter who can show emotions, this richness is increased even further.

Finally, you can easily retrieve past content if the presentation has been saved.

Consider this example. Donalda works for a cable provider. The main customer complaint is the two-day processing delay when ordering new cable packages. Her COO asks her to run a pilot project training her local telephone sales team to process orders. He also asks her to update senior executives, located around the country, on a regular basis.

Donalda considers the various communication platforms and settles on e-mail to make her reports. It allows her to be interactive while taking her time composing her messages.

She can attach any data she wants to share and can ensure senior executives receive the information quickly. As well, Donalda has a running record of all her e-mails to, and responses from, senior executives. For her situation, e-mail is the most appropriate platform choice.

Question

Match communication platforms to their characteristics. Platforms may match to more than one characteristic and each characteristic may have more than one match.

Options:

A. Phone
B. E-mail
C. Presentation with a facilitator
D. Text message
E. Instant messaging

Targets:

1. Highly interactive
2. Highly reliable
3. Limited capacity to convey rich messages
4. Retrievable content

Answer

Phone, e-mail, and presentations with facilitators are platforms that are interactive.

Highly reliable platforms include phone, presentations with facilitators, and instant messaging.

Text messages and instant messaging are limited when trying to convey rich messages. You're able to retrieve e-mail, presentation, and text message content.

USING ELEVATOR PITCHES AND PRESENTATIONS

Using elevator pitches and presentations

If you're faced with deciding which platform to use to communicate with senior executives, you'll likely choose a formal presentation. It offers many advantages, including an ability to convey a rich message and interactivity. But it's also wise to be prepared with an elevator pitch, in case you happen upon an opportunity to deliver it. Both platforms have guidelines that you should follow to use them effectively.

You already know that senior executives are busy, and scheduling a meeting with them to express a new idea is virtually impossible. An elevator pitch is a rare chance to make your speech face-to-face in the time it takes the elevator to get where it's going. To be sure you make a successful elevator pitch, there are four guidelines to follow: stick to the basics, avoid technical jargon, use buzz words, and narrow your approach.

Stick to the basics

Time is crucial in an elevator pitch, so stick to the basics and put your objective in perspective immediately. In other words, describe how the change will affect the organization as a whole – don't personalize it. Organize a set foundation of facts that gets to the heart of the matter right away.

For example, Jay clearly states in his elevator pitch that his objective is to make better products without spending more money.

Avoid technical jargon

Avoiding technical jargon should not be interpreted as "dumbing down" the material. Instead, by avoiding technical terms, you can get to your objective more quickly and leave the detailed decisions to be worked out later.

For example, Cindy avoids explaining during her elevator pitch how the end product is created and instead tells the CEO the problem is that the raw materials they use are of poor quality.

Use buzz words

Using buzz words puts your objective in focus. You should prepare your elevator pitch to suit the listener.

For example, Kevin uses the term "process improvement" in his elevator pitch because he knows the CEO is focused on that.

Narrow your approach

If you're serious about expressing your idea to a senior executive, then you'll find a way to narrow your approach and condense your message.

For example, Lauren's presentation can be condensed into one idea – changing the company's advertising to hit the right target market.

Question

Which statements are examples of people following the guidelines for an elevator pitch?

Options:

1. Chris states his objective right up front
2. Pat speaks about the business in general, not the technical side
3. Carey uses the words "budget constraints," as he knows that's a key concern for the CFO
4. Dawn feels so passionately about her idea, she can express it in just a few key statements
5. Carol explains the first of four phases in the short time she has
6. Frank explains the chemistry behind the process in highly technical terms

Answer

Option 1: This option is correct. When making your elevator pitch, the first thing you want to do is stick to the basics.

Option 2: This option is correct. Avoiding technical jargon will help you keep things simple and concise when preparing an elevator pitch.

Option 3: This option is correct. Using buzz words will help you tailor your elevator pitch to suit the executive you'll be speaking with and pique his interest.

Option 4: This option is correct. Narrowing your approach is an important guideline to help keep your elevator pitch concise and focused.

Option 5: This option is incorrect. When preparing an elevator pitch, time is crucial. You must get to the point and narrow your approach to make the most of your opportunity.

Option 6: This option is incorrect. When preparing an elevator pitch, you should avoid technical jargon.

As a manager, you know senior executives' time is valuable, so when making your formal presentation you want to make sure you use your time wisely. To ensure your success, you can follow six guidelines for effective formal presentations: follow the 10/20/30 rule, follow the 30 second rule, start with the reason for the presentation, present all options concisely, give clear recommendations, and summarize and give next steps.

When preparing your presentation, follow author and innovative thinker Guy Kawasaki's 10/20/30 rule. Ensure your presentation has no more than 10 slides and takes no more than 20 minutes to present, and use a 30-point font on your slides. An idea that's focused and concise will be able to fall within these boundaries.

An effective presentation should also follow the 30 second rule. Be prepared to present all your details in just 30 seconds. This ensures your objective is focused, and also prepares you if a senior executive gets called away a few minutes into your presentation.

When speaking, start with the reason for the presentation – to present information, get a decision, or have a discussion. Strive for clarity with a presentation that's logical and has flow. Senior executives want the main ideas, and time is always crucial, so be aware of the length and scope of your presentation. And make sure your information is precise; be brief, but have back-up information on hand.

Next you should present all options concisely, giving pros and cons such as company limitations, risks, financial gains or losses, resources necessary, and outlooks. An effective presentation should also include solutions or ideas for improvement. Keep in mind the audience's time and senior executives' availability.

Then, give clear recommendations based on the options that you think have the correct balance of pros and cons for the organization.

Finally, you should come to a clear conclusion, stating and agreeing on the next steps so everyone involved is aware of what's happening next in the process. For example, Gregor is giving a presentation about which team should take on an upcoming high-profile project. He presents the pros and cons of each team in less than 20 minutes and 10 slides.

Then he gives his recommendation. He discusses the next steps required and assigns each to a senior executive who verbally agrees to take it on. And he remains focused on his objective since when he prepared his presentation, he also followed the 30 second rule in case he only had time to express his main points.

Question

Which statements are examples of someone following the guidelines for delivering a presentation?

Options:

1. Eric begins by saying the presentation is to decide which consultant to hire, then he gives the pros and cons of each candidate

2. Eric gives his recommendation on the candidate that has the most pros and least cons and outlines the process for creating a consultant's contract

3. Eric manages to present all the information in 18 minutes with 10 large font slides, but he also prepares a 30-second condensed version

4. Eric tries to make all his points without using any technical terms

5. Eric makes a list of follow-up tasks and e-mails it out to the senior executives after the presentation

Answer

Option 1: This option is correct. You should begin with the reason for the presentation and then present all options concisely with pros and cons.

Option 2: This option is correct. When presenting you should give a clear recommendation and then summarize and give the next steps.

Option 3: This option is correct. It's important to follow both the 10/20/30 rule – 10 slides, less than 20 minutes, and a 30-point font – and the 30 second rule – present the main idea in 30 seconds or less.

Option 4: This option is incorrect. Avoiding technical jargon is a guideline for an effective elevator pitch.

Option 5: This option is incorrect. At the end of a presentation, you should summarize and give next steps while everyone is still attentive.

SECTION 3 - COMMUNICATING YOUR PURPOSE EFFECTIVELY

SECTION 3 - Communicating Your Purpose Effectively

Knowing how to effectively report and make proposals will add to your success in upward communication. When reporting, make sure you report only when you have something to convey or if you're going to miss a target. Always report the reasons for the delay.

When making a proposal, spell out the benefits and keep your message simple. Remember to appeal to the emotions of senior executives, and illustrate the performance improvement value of your idea.

REPORTING

Reporting

Communication is vital in business. If you've got a purpose for communicating with senior executives, such as reporting or proposing, you should be aware of the guidelines for each purpose. Following these guidelines will ensure you communicate your purpose successfully.

For example, you might be making some kind of a report, like a progress report on a project you're heading up.

Or you might be proposing a new initiative, new policy, or change, or trying to sell some other idea or product to senior executives at another organization.

Reporting to senior executives can be a one-time event – for example, to provide information about an upcoming initiative. Or it can be an ongoing process, such as scheduled status reports on a project. Either way, to ensure success there are three guidelines to follow when reporting: report only when there's something to report, report if you're missing a target, and report the reasons for the delay.

When there's something to report

You only need to supply reports if you have something significant to relay. Most senior executives are busy and their time is valuable. You can, however, submit a report that clearly notes that there's been no change since the last report. This ensures executives are updated without having to spend unnecessary time reading an unaltered report.

If you're missing a target

Be sure to make a report if you're going to miss a scheduled target. If you're not on schedule, or if a task hasn't been completed that should have been by now, you need to give senior executives a full report on why there's a delay.

The reasons for delay

If you're missing a target, you should focus on the reasons in your report – for example, the resignation of experienced staff members. The report must outline what the delay is, why it happened, the repercussions, and solutions.

Consider this example. Ralph is the safety manager at a manufacturing plant. He's changing safety procedures over a 12-month period to reduce employee injuries. Before beginning, Ralph and the senior executives agree on a reporting schedule of every three weeks. Since employees are on a three-week rotation, reporting would coincide with shift changes.

The first two reports have no changes, so Ralph suggests to senior executives that he only report if there's something significant going on.

Later, Ralph realizes that the next phase of the plan is going to be delayed due to the training of new employees.

Communicating Effectively with Senior Executives

He makes an early report, and the feedback from senior executives is positive. Ralph includes the reason for the delay in his report so everyone is clear on why the project is missing its target date.

Ralph followed the guidelines for reporting. At the beginning of the audit, there weren't any changes, so he decided not to report just for the sake of reporting on schedule. Then, when Ralph knew he was going to miss the next scheduled target, he made an early report. He alerted senior executives to the delay right away.

Finally, in his report, he explained the reason for the delay – that new staff members had to be trained before the project could continue.

Question

Ashley is managing the annual equipment maintenance and repair project.

Which examples illustrate Ashley following the appropriate guidelines for reporting to senior executives?

Options:

1. Ashley reports to senior executives every week, as changes are happening rapidly

2. Ashley makes an interim report when she realizes a parts shipment is delayed

3. Ashley explains in her report that the shipment is delayed due to a strike at the parts manufacturer

4. Ashley reports to the parts manufacturer how the delay affects her schedule

5. Ashley continues to report frequently to senior executives, even when there have been no changes

Answer

Option 1: This option is correct. Ashley reports often when she has significant information to report.

Option 2: This option is correct. Ashley makes an interim report when she knows the project will be delayed.

Option 3: This option is correct. Ashley makes sure her report covers the reason for the delay.

Option 4: This option is incorrect. Reporting to the parts manufacturer is not necessary or a part of the reporting guidelines.

Option 5: This option is incorrect. When following the appropriate guidelines for reporting, you should only report when you have significant information.

PROPOSING

Proposing

If you have a great initiative in mind, or a policy change you think might be good to implement, or if you're trying to sell senior executives on a new product or idea, you may find yourself making a proposal.

To achieve more successful upward communication, there are four guidelines for proposing: spell out the benefits, keep it simple, appeal to emotion, and show the performance improvement value.

Spell out the benefits

Spell out the benefits to senior executives when making a proposal. Clearly state how your proposal will improve the current situation, how difficult the change will be in reality, and how to make that change easier. Make sure you also have a backup plan in place for added security.

It's also important to ensure your proposal is in line with current senior executive thinking and organizational needs and goals. If your idea solves a problem that's currently on the senior executives' radar, you'll have a better chance of success.

Keep it simple

When communicating with senior executives, include no more than three points in your proposal. And show them you're an expert in your field by backing up your ideas with concrete facts and examples.

Appeal to emotion

Appealing to senior executives' emotions by relating personal experiences ensures your audience is engaged and helps prevent a bored or hostile reaction. Try to appeal to them through humor or find common areas you agree on.

Show performance improvement value

When proposing the value of your idea to senior executives, make sure you illustrate the performance improvement value. For example, a product has a value, and a product that improves a process has even greater value, but a product or process that increases the level of performance in a company has the greatest value of all.

Think back to Ralph at the manufacturing plant. He's proposing an idea that will lead to a decrease in injuries and an improvement in overall performance.

His presentation has three points – benefits, actions, and value. He explains the benefits concisely. Then he admits the change will be costly but points out that the budget is not yet decided, so it's a perfect time to factor in his idea.

He acknowledges that employees may resist, cracking a joke about how much he hates change himself, but he predicts that in the long run, plant performance will skyrocket. So Ralph followed the guidelines for making a proposal. He began by explaining the benefits, and he had a simple and concise presentation focused on just three points.

He appealed to the senior executives' emotions by sharing common budget and cost concerns and joking about resistance to change. And he made it clear that his proposed idea would not only decrease employee injuries, but also increase plant performance – it had performance improvement value.

Question

Everett manages a sales team for an office supply company. He makes a proposal for a budget increase in order to hire more employees.

Which examples illustrate Everett following the appropriate guidelines for making a proposal to senior executives?

Options:

1. Everett explains how additional sales employees will lead to increased profits

2. Everett's proposal points are simple – benefits, cost, and value

3. Everett proudly reminds senior executives how much the company has grown in the past five years

4. Everett clearly states that adding members to his sales team will increase the overall performance of the company

5. Everett makes interim reports leading up to his proposal

6. Everett makes his proposal via e-mail so he can attach sales forecasts

Answer

Option 1: This option is correct. Everett spells out the benefits to the company – increased profits – knowing this is something senior executives are interested in.

Option 2: This option is correct. Everett keeps it simple, using three points to make his proposal – benefits, cost, and value.

Option 3: This option is correct. Everett appeals to the emotions of senior executives by relating his pride in the growth of the company over a short time.

Option 4: This option is correct. Everett shows the performance improvement value of his idea to hire more sales staff members.

Option 5: This option is incorrect. Making interim reports to senior executives is not a part of making a proposal.

Option 6: This option is incorrect. Making a proposal via e-mail is not part of the guidelines for making a proposal to senior executives.

SECTION 4 - MAKING A REQUEST OF A SENIOR EXECUTIVE

SECTION 4 - Making a Request of a Senior Executive

Having the skills to successfully make a request of senior executives will help you develop your approach to upward communication. Begin by preparing your request ahead of time, and have solid facts to back you up. Then, follow the four steps that help you effectively make a request of senior executives.

The first step is to describe with clarity what you need. Next, describe exactly why you need it. Then, move on to explain what will happen if your request isn't fulfilled. And finally, describe the immediate and ongoing costs of what you're asking for.

MAKING A REQUEST

Making a request

As a manager, you have many reasons for upward communication, such as reporting or proposing. But another key purpose you might have for communicating with senior executives is to make a request.

You may find yourself making a request when you need additional resources, or permission to make a change, or more authority. Or you may need to ask for something more personal, such as a raise or promotion.

When preparing to make a request, take the time to do your homework. Decide what you're going to say, do all your calculations, and find evidence to back up your request. That way, when senior executives ask you for more detail, you'll be prepared.

When you're ready to conduct your meeting, there are four steps to follow that will help you make your request effectively:

1. clearly explain to senior executives exactly what you need,

2. give details on why you need what you're requesting,
3. clearly explain the consequences if you don't get what you're requesting, and
4. outline the cost of implementing your request and any continuing costs.

Step 1 – What

Step one involves explaining clearly what you need. For example, you might have to ask senior executives for additional resources to complete a project. You'd begin by clearly telling the senior executives that the additional resource you require is access to sensitive information.

This step can go wrong if you're not completely clear. For example, the resources granted to you could be inadequate because you weren't clear in the first place.

Step 2 – Why

Step two is to explain why you need what you're requesting. For example, you'd explain that additional access to information will make you more efficient and would enable you to do your job better and complete your project on time.

This might go wrong if you can't back up your argument for access to that information.

Step 3 – Consequences

Step three is to explain the consequences of not getting what you request. For example, you'd have to explain that if you don't have access to the sensitive information, your project may be over-budget or late.

This might go wrong if you enter the conversation expecting a fight, or if you're too emotional or hostile when stating your consequences.

Step 4 – Cost

Step four is to explain the immediate and ongoing cost to implement your request. For example, you'd have to outline how being granted access to the information you require could save money – keeping the project on budget.

This step could go wrong if you can't back up your information. You should ensure you've explored this avenue and can present a cost analysis to answer senior executives' questions regarding cost.

By following the four steps for making a request, you'll be more effective in asking senior executives for something you want.

Next, you'll have the opportunity to put your understanding into action as you make a request of a senior executive. You'll practice the four steps to effectively make your case.

REFERENCES

References

Planning and Leading Productive Meetings - 2001, Jeffrey H. Davis, Amacom

Quick! Show Me Your Value - 2004, Theresa Seagraves, ASTD

Project Management That Works: Real-World Advice on Communicating, Problem-Solving, and Everything Else You Need to Know to Get the Job Done - 2008, Rick A. Morris and Brette McWhorter Sember, AMACOM

Communications Skills for Project Managers - 2009, G. Michael Campbell, AMACOM

Painless Project Management: A Step-by-Step Guide for Planning, Executing and Managing Projects - 2007, Pamela McGhee and Peter McAliney, John Wiley & Sons

Power, Influence, and Persuasion: Sell Your Ideas and Make Things Happen - 2005, Harvard Business School Press, Harvard Business Press

Sorin Dumitrascu

Selling to the C-Suite: What Every Executive Wants You to Know About Successfully Selling to the Top - 2010, Nicholas A.C. Read and Stephen J. Bistritz , McGraw-Hill

GLOSSARY

Glossary

B

budget - The approved estimate for the project or any work breakdown structure (WBS) component or any schedule activity.

business communications - A collective term for an organization's marketing, advertising, branding, public relations and image management. The strategy for business communications is compiled in an organization's communications plan.

business drivers - People, knowledge, and conditions (e.g., market forces) that initiate and support activities for which the business was designed. A driver is most commonly a factor that contributes to the growth of a particular business.

C

communication platform - A method of communication by which a message is relayed. Platforms allow you to deliver messages face-to-face or electronically.

communications - See business communications.

E

electronic chat - Typed conversations that occur in real time. Text is displayed in a chat window on each participant's desktop monitor. More than two people may participate in a chat session, if desired.

elevator pitch - A term used to refer to a brief opportunity to speak with a senior executive. The idea or pitch must be communicated in the time it takes an elevator to take the senior executive to the destination.

G

guideline - A suggested principle, recommendation, procedure, or best practice for application in a particular circumstance.

I

instant messaging - A form of communication via typed text in real time over the Internet.

O

objective - Something toward which work is to be directed, a strategic position to be attained, a purpose to be achieved, a result to be obtained, a product to be produced, or a service to be performed.

opportunity - A condition or situation favorable to the project, a positive set of circumstances, a positive set of events, a risk that will have a positive impact on project objectives, or a possibility for positive changes.

P

problem-solving meeting - A meeting used to discuss and remedy situations that are affecting, or that have the potential to affect, the outcome or output of a project or initiative.

T

team members - The people assigned to do the work required to complete a project or initiative.

teleconference - An electronic meeting between two or more groups in different locations using audio, video, and computer systems.

teleconferencing - A meeting conducted via telephone.

text messaging - A form of communication most commonly using cell phones or similar devices. Brief text messages are typed and sent via a network.

time management - The process of planning, recording, and quantifying time spent completing tasks.

U

upward communication - Communication with a higher level in the hierarchy of a company, such as managers to senior executives.

V

videoconferencing - The use of communication technologies to exchange digitized video images and audio between two or more separate sites, with the purpose of allowing participants to see, hear and collaborate in real-time.

W

web conferencing - A meeting conducted over the Internet.

web conferencing software - Online technology that allows people in different locations to conduct meetings and share information through their personal computers.

www.ingramcontent.com/pod-product-compliance
Lightning Source LLC
Chambersburg PA
CBHW020928180526
45163CB00007B/2925